# Growing Up in Saudi Arabia

**Other titles in the *Growing Up Around the World* series include:**

# Growing Up in Saudi Arabia

Barbara Sheen

ReferencePoint
Press®

San Diego, CA

© 2018 ReferencePoint Press, Inc.
Printed in the United States

**For more information, contact:**
ReferencePoint Press, Inc.
PO Box 27779
San Diego, CA 92198
www. ReferencePointPress.com

LIBRARY OF CONGRESS CATALOGING-IN-PUBLICATION DATA

Name: Sheen, Barbara, author.
Title: Growing Up in Saudi Arabia/by Barbara Sheen.
Description: San Diego, CA: ReferencePoint Press, Inc., 2017. | Series:
    Growing Up Around the World series | Includes bibliographical references
    and index.
Identifiers: LCCN 2017041094 (print) | LCCN 2017048332 (ebook) | ISBN
    9781682823248 (eBook) | ISBN 9781682823231 | ISBN 9781682823231 (hardback)
Subjects: LCSH: Saudi Arabia—Social life and customs—21st century. | Saudi
    Arabia—Religious life and customs. | Families—Saudi Arabia. |
    Education—Saudi Arabia.
Classification: LCC DS215 (ebook) | LCC DS215 .S47 2017 (print) | DDC
    953.805/4—dc23
LC record available at https://lccn.loc.gov/2017041094

# CONTENTS

# SAUDI ARABIA AT A GLANCE

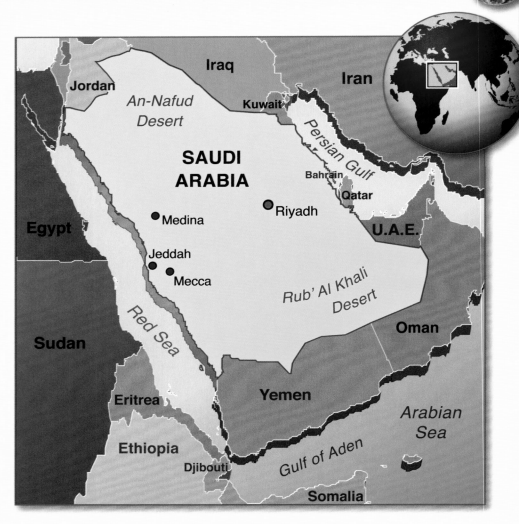

**Official Name**
Kingdom of Saudi Arabia

**Capital** ●
Riyadh

**Size**
829,999 square miles
(2,149,688 sq. km)

**Total Population** ●
28,160,273 as of July 2016

**Youth Population**
0–14 years: 25.56%
15–24 years: 18.85%

**Religion** ●
Islam

**Type of Government**
Absolute monarchy

**Language**
Arabic

**Currency**
Riyal

**Industries**
Crude oil production, oil
refining, petrochemicals,
industrial gases, ammonia,
cement, fertilizer, ship and
airplane repair, construction,
agriculture

**Literacy** ●
94.7% (age 15+ able
to read and write)

**Internet Users**
19.32 million, or 69.6%
of the population

# CHAPTER ONE

# A Mix of Modern and Traditional

Saudi Arabia is a nation that is both extremely modern and deeply traditional. In a relatively short time, it has gone from being a poor, undeveloped nation to one of the most materially modern countries in the world. Until the middle of the twentieth century, Saudi Arabia did not have modern roads, widespread electricity, or formal schooling for girls, and slavery was legal. In contrast, contemporary Saudi Arabia is home to high-tech research centers, world-class universities, superhighways, and sophisticated desalinization plants. As a Saudi man explains, "Less than thirty years ago, my peers and I did not own shoes. Now we must own a luxury car to look modern and important."[1]

Funding for modernization projects derives from oil-production profits. With one-quarter of the earth's oil reserves, Saudi Arabia is the world's second-largest oil producer and is home to some of the world's most advanced technology for oil and gas exploration and production. Saudi Arabia is also the birthplace of Islam and the spiritual center of the Muslim faith. Islam's two holiest shrines, the Sacred Mosque and the Prophet's Mosque, are located in the cities of Mecca and Medina, respectively. The nation is responsible for caring for these sacred sites and preserving the ancient traditions they represent. In fact, all of the nation's laws are based on Wahhabism, a fourteen-hundred-year-old, deeply conservative branch of Islam.

The government has worked hard to ensure that modernization efforts do not weaken the nation's traditional values. Material development related to education, health care, defense, infrastructure, and technology is supported. But aspects of Western culture that are believed to lead to vice, thereby weakening

Islamic values, are prohibited. For example, there are no movie theaters, bars, or nightclubs in the nation, and publications and websites are censored. As teenager Saad explains, "Saudi society had every type of [peaceful] revolution except social. It had an agricultural and economic revolution, but people's mentality did not change."[2]

The mingling of traditional and modern is apparent to residents and visitors alike. "From a Western point of view, the Kingdom of Saudi Arabia is a land of contrasts," author Ann T. Jordan wrote in 2011. "There is a seemingly strong contrast between the ultra-modern shopping center and the traditional dress of the shoppers, between the twenty-first century quality of the traffic jam and the fact that all the drivers are males because women are not allowed to drive."[3] In another modernizing step, in September 2017 the Saudi government issued a decree making it legal for women to drive by June 2018. Indeed, the conflicting aspects of Saudi Arabian culture have a big impact on the lives of its youth.

*A Saudi family relaxes at a beach on the Persian Gulf. To outsiders, the traditional* niqab *head covering worn by this woman might seem an unusual garment for beachgoers, but Saudis are comfortable enjoying modern-day pursuits while respecting age-old customs.*

## Geography

Saudi Arabia is a large country located on the Arabian Peninsula in the Middle East. It borders Jordan, Iraq, and Kuwait to the north; Qatar, the United Arab Emirates, Oman, and Yemen to the south; the Red Sea to the west; and the Persian Gulf to the east. It is also connected via a causeway to Bahrain, which is located off Saudi Arabia's Gulf coast.

With a total area of 829,999 square miles (2,149,688 sq. km), it is the fourteenth-largest country in the world. Much of the terrain consists of deserts, but the nation also has extensive coastline along the Persian Gulf and the Red Sea. There are no permanent rivers or lakes in the country. Instead, there are wadis, or dry riverbeds, that fill up when it rains—which is not often. Some areas can go for years without any rainfall. Consequently, until recently only a small part of the nation could be farmed. Modern water transportation and storage technologies, however, have transformed large areas of the desert into agricultural land where grains, fruits, and vegetables are cultivated.

## A Burdensome Past

Although most young Saudis either were children or were not yet born when the September 11, 2001 (also known as 9/11), terror attacks on the United States occurred, the event has left a mark on them. Fifteen of the nineteen men involved in the attacks, which killed 2,996 people and injured more than 6,000 others, were Saudis. They were members of al Qaeda, a radical Islamist group. At that time, the leader of al Qaeda was a wealthy Saudi businessman named Osama bin Laden. He believed that the West in general and the United States in particular were intent on destroying Islamic values throughout the world. He recruited young Muslim men and boys, many of whom were Saudis, to join al Qaeda and fight this threat. He urged his followers to attack the United States and other Western nations.

Although the Saudi government cracked down on radical groups operating within its borders after 9/11, many Westerners believe that Saudi Arabia is a nation that encourages terrorism. As a result, young Saudis are frequently perceived as potential terrorists and are treated suspiciously when they travel or study in the United States and Europe.

Whereas rainstorms are rare, haboobs—massive sand-storms driven by heavy winds—are common. Walls of blowing sand drastically reduce visibility and present health risks for vulnerable individuals, such as children with asthma. Sometimes these storms are so severe that schools, businesses, and roads are closed.

Extreme heat in the summer, when temperatures can soar to 129°F (54°C), is also common. Says Kristine, a Canadian blogger who lives in Saudi Arabia, "It's hot most of the year. By hot I mean melt your mascara to your face kinda hot through the summer months."[4]

## History

Although the area that makes up modern Saudi Arabia has been inhabited for at least fifteen thousand years, for most of its history it has not been unified. It was split into four regions, which were further divided among various warring tribes ruled by tribal chiefs known as sheikhs and emirs. Trade routes that connected Asia and the Middle East crisscrossed the land, and cities developed along these routes. The founder of the Muslim religion, the prophet Muhammad, was born in Mecca, one of these cities.

Muhammad believed that he received a series of revelations from God. These became the basis for the Muslim religion and for the Koran, Islam's holy book. Islam soon became the dominant religion in the region. But despite sharing a common religion, the tribes continued to battle each other for centuries. Not until 1932 did a sheikh, Abdul Aziz ibn Saud, unify the nation and become its first king. Shortly thereafter, oil was discovered. The government established an oil company in conjunction with Standard Oil of California named the Arabian-American Oil Company (Aramco). Soon thousands of Americans entered the country to work in the oil industry. At first, oil revenues were not significant; however, worldwide oil prices increased dramatically during the 1970s, making Saudi Arabia one of world's richest nations.

Using this newfound wealth, the government set out to modernize the nation without compromising its religious values. As author and King Saud University sociology professor M.A. Nezami explains, "Cadillacs replaced camel[s] . . . super highways cut across the vast sandy deserts, and ultra-modern buildings and supermarkets mush-roomed in cities and towns."[5]

As time passed, many Saudis came to re-sent sharing control of Aramco with its Ameri-can partner. In 1988 the Saudi government purchased the company, renaming it the Sau-di Arabian Oil Company—popularly known as Saudi Aramco. It is one of the world's largest and most valuable companies, extracting 10 million barrels of oil a day and earning Saudi Arabia the equivalent of $205.2 billion annu-ally. The government uses a large percentage of this money to fund ongoing modernization projects. It also pays for a generous social welfare program that most young people depend on to subsidize their income, educa-tion, and health care, among other things.

## Royal Rule

The Kingdom of Saudi Arabia is an absolute monarchy, with Islam as the state religion. In this form of government, a monarch has supreme authority over a nation and its people. The position of king is determined by heredity. The current king, Salman bin Ab-dulaziz Al Saud, is the son of King Abdul Aziz ibn Saud and the head of the House of Saud, the Saudi royal family. His official title is King of Saudi Arabia and Custodian of the Two Mosques.

Saudi Arabia has three branches of government: executive, legislative, and judicial. Members of all three branches are ap-pointed by the king and include many members of the Al Saud family. The nation is divided into thirteen provinces, each with its own local government. The governors (twelve of whom are princ-es) and half of the members of each local provincial council are selected by the king. In an attempt to modernize the government, in 2005 men age twenty-one and older were granted the right to vote for the remaining council members, as were women in 2015.

Otherwise, Saudis have few civil liberties. There is no right to assemble or right to free speech; secret police charged with maintaining national security arrest people who are publicly critical of the government. "In this country, if you open your mouth, you end up in prison,"[6] says Mohammad al Qahtani, a Saudi human rights activist.

The Koran serves as the nation's constitution, and all Saudi laws are derived from religious leaders' interpretation of Islamic doctrine. This is known as sharia law. Sharia law affects almost every aspect of a person's life, covering issues related to religious practices, dress, gender equality, education, social practices, and sexuality, among other things. Many of the freedoms that Western teens take for granted do not exist. For example, starting at puberty, females must cover their bodies from head to toe in public. They are required to wear a headscarf and an *abaya*—a loose-fitting, full-length cloak—over their regular clothes. The abaya, according to a female medical student, "represents respect for my community and preserving my culture."[7] Although not required by law, many women wear a *niqab* instead of a scarf. This garment covers the wearer's head and face, except for the eyes.

*These women at a shopping mall in Riyadh wear long, flowing abayas, full-body coverings that are prescribed under sharia law.*

Other laws separate the sexes. Men and women can mingle only if they are family members or a married couple. Unrelated boys and girls are forbidden from socializing with each other or even sharing the same social space. Actions as seemingly innocent as an unrelated man and woman walking near each other or having coffee together are strictly forbidden. Schools, universities, public facilities, and businesses are segregated by gender. For example, libraries, banks, and restaurants either have men-only and women-only branches or two distinct sections, one for males and one for families, which includes women. As Jordan explains,

> Public spaces allow for the separation of the sexes. . . . Restaurants often have two sections: one for men and the other for families; women eat in the family section, whether eating with their families or with female friends. In McDonald's, for example, each table in the family section is curtained off. This allows women to remove their face veils when dining without concern that men who are not close relatives will see them.[8]

Morality police, known as the *mutaween*, monitor public areas looking for lawbreakers who, depending on their particular offense, may be reprimanded, fined, beaten with a stick or whip, or imprisoned.

## A Young Population

Saudi Arabia's population is young and growing. During the 1960s the country had a population of about 4 million people. In comparison, the current population is 28,160,273. Most are younger than thirty, and about 45 percent are under twenty-five. The national language is Arabic, although English is a popular second language.

Ethnically, 90 percent of Saudi citizens are Arabs, and 10 percent are Afro-Asian. Although not citizens, about 30 percent of the population consists of foreign workers. Many are unskilled laborers from Southeast Asia and the Middle East. They do manual labor, work in stores and restaurants, and serve as

## Oil, Social Welfare, and Saudi Youth

Young Saudis depend on generous social welfare benefits provided by the government to subsidize their lifestyles. Funds for these benefits come from oil sales. However, in recent years the price of oil has declined while Saudi Arabia's population has increased. As a result, although there are more young people expecting to be helped by welfare benefits, the government has less money to spend.

An article by Kate Drew for CNBC explains:

> If Saudi Arabia maintains oil production at current levels amid the oil price crash, then it's going to have to cut its budget. . . . The big issue is Saudi Arabia's big spending ways especially increased government spending on social welfare programs. . . . The House of Saud provides its citizens with housing, education, health care—even electricity tariffs tend to be low. . . . Saudi citizens are not subject to a personal income tax and enjoy perks like subsidized gasoline. . . . In February [2015] . . . King Salman doled out a reported $32 billion to the Saudi people in bonuses and subsidies to celebrate his ascension to the throne.

As of 2016, the Saudi government was tapping into cash reserves to help fund these programs. However, many young Saudis believe cuts in social benefits, which they fear will negatively affect their future financial security, are inevitable.

Kate Drew, "Saudi Arabia's Big Welfare Spending Faces the Oil Abyss," CNBC, December 3, 2015. www.cnbc.com.

drivers and household servants. Others are skilled professionals from the United States and Europe who are employed by Saudi Aramco, private businesses, universities, and hospitals. Young Saudis interact with these foreigners and are often influenced by them.

### Cities and Towns

One of the biggest changes in Saudi Arabia is the growth of its cities. Until about sixty years ago most Saudis lived in rural areas. Today, about 83 percent of Saudis live in urban areas. The kingdom has four cities with a population of more than 1 million people, including the capital of Riyadh, home to 6.1 million, many of whom are youngsters. Saudi cities are bustling places where modernization projects are ongoing. As Jordan explains, "Every time I make a trip to Riyadh, it strikes me as a city under construction. There are new skyscrapers in the city center and new houses under construction in the suburbs. Much of the compact, old mud-brick city . . . is gone, replaced by a new city of spread-out, marble and concrete buildings and wide streets requiring vehicle transportation."[9]

Ultramodern buildings are everywhere, often in close proximity to world-famous mosques. Every neighborhood has at least one mosque, and loudspeakers call Saudis to prayer five times a day. There are also lots of parks where families gather for picnics after the sun goes down and temperatures drop. Lavish royal palaces set behind high walls stretch for blocks. There are also middle-class and poorer neighborhoods.

Western fast-food eateries, high-end boutiques, and megamalls abound. Besides containing hundreds of shops, most malls have cafés and restaurants, banks, and children's playgrounds. Some have a conference center, hotel, offices, and apartments located within them. One mall even has an indoor ski slope equipped with artificial snow. As Oceana, an American teen living in Saudi Arabia, explains, "The malls here make any mall in the U.S look poor."[10]

Out on the street, the traffic is frenetic. Motorists often drive in reverse, switch lanes, jump onto the curb to pass, tailgate, and sideswipe each other like racecars. Trucks carrying camels vie for space alongside Lamborghinis. All the drivers are male. (The new law permitting women drivers is not slated to take effect until June 2018.) Some are underage, unlicensed boys whose feet barely reach the pedals. According to Tiffany Wacaser, an American blogger living in Saudi Arabia, "People disregard traffic rules. They turn a 5 lane into a 10 lane road. Turns are made from anywhere the driver wants to be. It is insane. . . . I've seen a number of boys who look younger than my 13-year-old son driving their mothers around . . . [and] kids hanging out windows, bouncing around on the seats, and babies sitting on fathers' laps at the steering wheel."[11]

> "Every time I make a trip to Riyadh, it strikes me as a city under construction. There are new skyscrapers in the city center and new houses under construction in the suburbs."[9]
>
> —Ann T. Jordan, author

Riyadh, the capital of Saudi Arabia, has undergone rapid growth in recent decades. It still has ancient markets and traditional neighborhoods, but office skyscrapers, shopping centers, and luxury hotels—along with automobile congestion—now dominate the downtown districts.

Pedestrian traffic is much more sedate. The heat keeps many people indoors during the daytime, and those who are out segregate by gender unless they are with a family member. Under sharia law, females are required to either be escorted by a male family member when they go out in public or to have permission from their guardian to go out without an escort. "We're not allowed to even go to the supermarket without permission or a companion, and that's a simple thing on the huge, horrendous list of rules we have to follow,"[12] explains a young woman.

Almost everyone dresses uniformly. All the women wear black abayas and some type of head covering. Many also cover their faces. Most of the men wear *thobes*—traditional, long flowing white robes—paired with a long red-and-white checkered cloth draped over their heads. Janet Breslin-Smith, the wife of a former US ambassador to Saudi Arabia, describes the effect this uniformity has on the city of Riyadh: "On one level, it looks like any modern city. But as your eyes gaze down to people walking, it almost takes you back to biblical times. People are dressed as they have for thousands of years."[13]

Two of Saudi Arabia's cities, Mecca and Medina, are distinct. Under Saudi law, non-Muslims are prohibited from entering either city. Authorities stationed at checkpoints make sure that the law is enforced. Therefore, young people who live in these cities do not have regular contact with non-Muslims, but they do have lots of contact with Muslims from other countries who flock to these cities on religious pilgrimages.

> "It's good here. We can't criticize the king and the princes, but things are getting better. We have restrictions; we know that. But we're cool."[14]
>
> —Hussein, a young Saudi man

Outside the cities, except for telltale electrical wires, satellite dishes, and late-model cars, rural villages appear rooted in the past. In fact, some rural residents live in much the same way as their tribal ancestors did. About 10 percent of Saudis are Bedouins who live in the desert and earn their living raising camels, sheep, and goats. These nomadic people do not reside in a permanent place. Instead, they migrate seasonally, living in large tents that they move among grazing lands. But modernization has affected them too. Most have cell phones and pickup trucks, which they drive on modern paved roads that connect desert towns and cities.

## Moving into the Future

Like all nations, the Kingdom of Saudi Arabia faces challenges as it moves into the future. For many young Saudis, one of the greatest challenges is finding a balance between the modern world and traditional values. Some young people want their nation to change faster, particularly in the areas of women's rights and civil liberties, but still respect tradition. In contrast, others believe that further modernization efforts will put Islamic values at risk. Many of these young people support tighter religious restrictions and less contact with non-Muslim nations. Still other young Saudis are satisfied with the status quo. Hussein is one of these young people. "It's good here," he says. "We can't criticize the king and the princes, but things are getting better. We have restrictions; we know that. But we're cool."[14]

Clearly, Saudi youths have differing opinions about what direction their nation should take as it moves into the future. But no matter what sort of balance is achieved, their numbers alone ensure that they will be integral in shaping that future. As Salman, a young Saudi man, explains, "There are tensions here between modernity and tradition . . . but the wheel of evolution will not stop, cannot stop turning."[15]

# CHAPTER TWO

# Family Ties

Family and family ties are the bedrock of Saudi society. Youngsters are brought up to respect, obey, and rely on their parents. As Said, a young man, explains, "I want to be just like my father. I admire his wisdom, his reactions and the way he handles problems. There is so much to learn from the older generation."[16] Parents and extended family members have a huge influence on the lives of young Saudis.

### The Nuclear Family

By law, Saudi men are allowed to have four wives. However, this practice is on the decline. Most Saudis grow up in a traditional nuclear family that consists of a father, mother, and siblings. As recently as ten years ago Saudis often married in their teens, and there are still cases of arranged marriages between girls who have barely reached puberty and older men. However, with more young people focused on getting an education, most Saudis are marrying later. Currently, the average age of marriage is twenty-six, and, on average, couples have three children.

> "I want to be just like my father. I admire his wisdom, his reactions and the way he handles problems. There is so much to learn from the older generation."[16]
>
> —Said, a young Saudi man

Saudi families are patriarchal in structure. The father is the chief decision maker, provider, and protector of the family. His authority is absolute. Children are expected to respect and obey him without question. Indeed, although it is uncommon, individuals can be imprisoned for disobeying their fathers. As one young Saudi male recalls,

"While growing up my main concern was to obey. . . . There was no discussion. You just obey."[17]

Mothers are charged with raising the children and running the household. They, too, are expected to be submissive to their husbands. "My mother told me to respect a man: If your husband says milk is black, you must agree,"[18] explains Saudi anthropologist Salwa Abdel Hammeed al Khateeb.

Patriarchy and male dominance are promoted by the nation's culture and laws. For instance, a man can divorce his wife by simply saying "I divorce you" three times. In contrast, if a woman wants to end a marriage, she must go through a long, complex court battle. And if a couple divorces, the law automatically grants custody of the children to the father.

Saudi families are still dominated by the will of the father. This does not mean that most fathers are strict or intolerant. Saudis love their families, and Saudi fathers want to see their children succeed and enjoy fulfilling lives.

## Guardianship

One reason for male dominance in Saudi Arabia is that by tradition females are considered to be the weaker sex, both physically and emotionally. Males, therefore, must safeguard them. Considering these cultural norms, it is not surprising that girls are raised to be more docile than their brothers, and they are more sheltered. As teenager Muna explains, "As the only girl in the family I was treated very strictly. My parents allowed my brothers to go out after school while I had to sit and wait for some of our relatives to visit us."[19]

> "A father controls every aspect of a Saudi girl's life until she is passed to a new dominant male—her husband."[20]
>
> —Karen Elliot House, author

According to author Karen Elliot House, "A father controls every aspect of a Saudi girl's life until she is passed to a new dominant male—her husband."[20] From birth to death, all Saudi females are required to have a male guardian. This person is charged with looking out for her welfare and protecting her honor. Guardians supervise almost every aspect of their charge's life. They are empowered to make a wide range of important decisions on her behalf, even if she disagrees with these decisions.

Usually a woman's father, brother, husband, or son serves as her guardian. Girls and women cannot leave the house, study, work, travel, marry, divorce, sign legal documents, or obtain some forms of medical care without their guardian's consent. Some women like being watched over in this manner. Oum is one of these women. "I like that I have a guardian who looks out for me and cares for my well-being and defends me and takes on what I can't handle,"[21] she says.

Others, like nineteen-year-old Bashayr, find the practice oppressive. She comments, "It's like I'm in handcuffs, and the society, the law, the people [are] against us."[22]

## Support and Dependence

Although boys are not as closely supervised as their sisters, they, too, depend on their parents for financial and emotional support. Parents typically provide for their children's every material need until they marry.

Wealthy families often buy their sons luxury cars and their daughters expensive clothes and jewelry. Emotionally, Saudi parents are closely involved in helping their children make major life decisions, such as selecting a career and choosing a spouse. It is up to a boy's mother to seek out a prospective wife for him. She usually does this with the help of other female relatives, friends, or a professional matchmaker. Rasha Alduwaisi, who married the son of one of her mother's coworkers, recalls her experience: "My mother had a good friend at work. She had a son who . . . thought it was time to start a family. So he asked his mom for help. She started 'searching' for a wife. . . . She thought to ask my mother if any of her daughters was ready for marriage simply because she thought she [Alduwaisi's mother] was a decent well-educated person."[23]

Once a suitable prospect is found, the bride's father makes inquiries about the prospective groom's character. If the bride's father approves of the match, the boy is invited to meet the girl in the presence of her guardian. Typically, her face is covered during this initial meeting. In some cases, especially in more conservative families, the couple does not meet until the wedding, but they are given information about each other. If they agree to wed, the

Wealthy fathers often spoil their sons and daughters with luxury goods partly to show how well they can provide for their children.

two fathers negotiate a marriage contract that covers a range of financial details. Once the marriage contract is signed, the couple is engaged, and they are allowed to have limited contact with each other under the supervision of the girl's guardian. In other instances, the prospective bride and groom have already met, usually while traveling or studying abroad or at a family gathering. In fact, an estimated 60 percent of marriages in Saudi Arabia are between cousins. In cases where the couple has already met, the prospective groom shares his interest with his mother, and the families begin the process of arranging a marriage. In either scenario, individuals rarely marry anyone who does not meet with their parents' approval. Indeed, by law women cannot marry without their guardian's consent.

## Extended Family Relations

When individuals marry, their families become entwined. In-laws join each other's extended family, and the families become connected forever. Most Saudis grow up with extremely close ties to their extended families. Author and former diplomat David E.

## Family Honor

Family honor is very important in Saudi Arabian culture. From an early age, youngsters are expected to live up to socially prescribed values and act in a way that maintains the family's honor. Girls bring honor to their families if they are modest, chaste, respectful, selfless, and devout. Boys are expected to be generous, devout, hospitable, and honest. Once they marry, boys are expected to be good providers. If boys and girls do not exhibit these characteristics, the whole family is humiliated and dishonored, which lowers its status in society.

It is the job of Saudi males to maintain their family's honor. This role is taken so seriously that it is not uncommon for young boys to reprimand their sisters and even their mother if the women are doing something that is considered immodest, such as not completely covering their hair in public.

Respect for others is crucial in maintaining family honor. Insulting a family elder, a man's mother, or a person's tribe can lead to feuds that last for decades.

Long explains that "the extended family is the single most important structural unit of society in Saudi Arabia; virtually every Saudi considers themselves members of an extended family. Each family member shares a collective ancestry, a collective respect for elders, and a collective obligation and responsibility for the welfare of the other family members."[24]

Extended family groups can number into the thousands. For example, the Al Saud family comprises approximately thirty thousand people. One reason why extended family groups are so large is because most Saudis can trace their family tree back hundreds of years through tribal lines. Although young Saudis may not know everyone in their extended family, they usually have a close relationship with their grandparents, aunts, uncles, and cousins. In fact, it is common for three or four generations of extended family members to live close to each other and for first cousins to grow up together. Even faraway family members stay in frequent touch via telephone and the Internet, and they make a point of attending family events whenever possible.

> "The extended family is the single most important structural unit of society in Saudi Arabia; virtually every Saudi considers themselves members of an extended family."[24]
>
> —David E. Long, an author and retired US Foreign Service officer

Large family gatherings occur frequently. At these events, family members segregate by gender. Some of these gatherings occur at the homes of older relatives. Saudi culture esteems the elderly. Most teens have close relationships with family elders, and they enjoy these visits.

Old or young, Saudi families look out for each other. They help each other out financially, go into business together, celebrate life events together, and comfort each other during bad times. For example, when her brother died suddenly, a young Saudi woman was consoled and supported by her cousins, who visited her almost every day. "[Family] is such a comfort in hard times," she explains, "and it is my family that has gotten me through this crisis."[25]

## A Variety of Homes

Young Saudis grow up in a variety of homes. The type and size of the home depends on the location and the family's income, ranging from royal palaces to canvas tents. But the majority of young Saudis grow up in comfortable apartments in modern high-rise buildings or in well-appointed attached or freestanding homes known as villas. Often, multiple family groups live in a compound that consists of three or four neighboring villas enclosed by a tall wall. For example, two brothers and their wives and children might live in adjacent villas, while their parents and unmarried adult siblings occupy a third villa. Generally, all the homes in a compound open onto a common outdoor area with a fragrant garden, a tinkling fountain, palm trees, and often a swimming pool. Some affluent families often set up a luxurious tent furnished with hanging lanterns, thick carpets, and plush cushions in the outdoor area. It serves as a retreat where young male family members hang out and entertain friends.

Almost all Saudi homes are surrounded by a high wall. Privacy is very important to Saudis. The wall muffles street noise, protects children from traffic, keeps out litter, and, most importantly, shields the family, particularly the women, from public view. Similarly, windows in houses and apartments that can be seen from the street are covered with film or are boarded over so that no one can see in. As author Nicholas Buchele points out, "Saudis are unusually jealous of their family's privacy. The joke goes that on a building site the wall around the plot is the first thing to go up and this is generally true. The windows of family homes, however distant from the neighbors, are invariably mirrored glass or blacked out."[26]

Most homes are made from sun-dried mud bricks and have multiple rounded archways both inside and out. There are usually two distinct entrances—one for males and one for females—that lead to separate male and female quarters. It is in these quarters that same-sex guests are entertained. The men's quarters are usually located on the ground floor, and the women's quarters are tucked away on an upper floor so that unveiled women cannot be seen by male visitors. Each of these quarters contains a sitting room. Some also contain bedrooms. The sitting room is usually furnished with cushioned benches running along the walls as well as Western-style living and dining room furniture. Almost all Saudi homes have electricity and indoor plumbing. Most have modern appliances, air conditioning, and Internet access. Satellite dishes dot almost every roof.

The homes of poor families are usually smaller than those of more affluent individuals, and furnishings are minimal. Poor teens may share a bedroom and, frequently, a bed with same-gender siblings. Some sleep on pallets that are rolled up during the day and then unrolled at night. In contrast, middle-class and wealthy teens usually have their own bedrooms that resemble those of Western teens. As a Saudi teen explains, "Saudi Arabia is not like you'd think in Hollywood movies like Ali Baba and the 40 Thieves or Aladdin. . . . We live in modern houses, with satellite TV, flat screen TVs, mobile phones, automatic kitchen appliances like microwaves, dishwashers, fridges, etc. . . . Our houses have the same stuff yours does . . . couches, lamps, rugs, a/c."[27]

## Food

No matter what type of home teens grow up in, mealtimes typically feature an abundance of tasty food. And guests are always welcome. Hospitality is an important part of Islamic culture. Saudis almost always have mint tea, spiced coffee, chocolate, and dates on hand to serve to visitors upon their arrival.

*A group of Saudi men gather to eat a meal of goat meat and rice. Sharing food with others is a common expression of Saudi hospitality.*

Traditionally, Arabs eat with their right hand while seated on cushions around a cloth spread on the floor. Although some people still follow this tradition, most use cutlery and sit on chairs around a dining room table. Food is abundant in Saudi Arabia. What is served depends on the family, but certain foods are prohibited by Islamic dietary laws. Forbidden foods include pork, fish that do not have scales, carnivorous animals, animals that are not slaughtered in a humane manner, and alcoholic beverages. Prohibited foods are not sold in Saudi stores.

Saudi cities and towns have modern supermarkets as well as traditional maze-like shopping complexes that are known as souks. These contain hundreds of shops and stalls that sell all kinds of foods in addition to other merchandise. Usually, the lady

## Women's Freedom

Regardless of their age, all Saudi females must have a male guardian. This is usually a girl's father, with the role passing to her husband when she marries. If she does not marry, the role usually passes to her brother upon her father's death. A son usually serves as the guardian of a widow or divorcee.

Opponents of the guardianship system say that it restricts a woman's freedom and treats her like a minor all her life. Some Saudi women have taken to social media to campaign against the system. According to a report posted on CNN, "Some, dressed in abayas, post selfies holding signs with short messages like, 'Slavery comes in many shapes and forms: Male guardianship is one.' And because they are prohibited from traveling without their guardian's permission, others post pictures of the cover of their Saudi passport with statements like, 'I'm a prisoner and my crime is that I'm a Saudi woman.'"

The campaign has garnered support from people all over the world. Saudi Arabia's most senior religious leader, however, is not among the supporters. He favors the guardianship system and calls the campaign a "crime targeting the Saudi and Muslim society."

In contrast, the organization Human Rights Watch says that "the practice of male guardianship in its many forms impairs and in some cases nullifies women's exercise of a host of human rights." The women vow to continue the campaign until the male guardianship system is outlawed.

Donie O'Sullivan, "The Women Tweeting for Their Freedom in Saudi Arabia," CNN, September 16, 2016. www.cnn.com.

of the house shops for food accompanied by a female servant and a male escort. According to Buchele, "In the supermarket, [the lady of the house] will simply point at the goods while the maid stocks the cart or, in the souk, picks up the bags."[28]

In most homes, a servant prepares the meals. Saudis pray five times a day, and mealtimes are largely determined by the daily prayer schedule. Breakfast is eaten after dawn prayers. Youngsters, in a hurry to get to school, often eat breakfast alone. A typical breakfast might consist of tea or coffee, yogurt, eggs, goat cheese, and flatbread spread with a mashed garbanzo bean dish called hummus. Lunch is usually eaten anytime between 2:00 and 6:00 p.m., following midafternoon prayers. Families usually eat lunch together. The school day is over, and most businesses close their doors during this time, only to reopen later. So lunchtime is the perfect time for parents and children to relax and enjoy a meal together.

No matter what else is served, the meal is likely to contain fresh, hot flatbread. Indeed, no meal is complete in Saudi Arabia without bread. Rice is also very popular. A common main dish is a rice casserole called *kabsa,* which contains lamb, chicken, or fish with rice, tomatoes, vegetables, and spices. It is served with flatbread, salad, and yogurt and is followed by a dessert of fresh fruit or a delicious syrup-coated pastry.

Supper is a light meal that is eaten quite late, typically between 10:00 p.m. and 2:00 a.m. Saudi Arabia comes alive during these late hours when outdoor temperatures drop and the final evening prayers are finished. In fact, it is common for families to go out for supper after midnight at one of the many foreign-owned fast-food chains that are so popular in the nation. For instance, when blogger Tiffany Wacaser and her husband went out for supper in Riyadh at 8:00 p.m., the restaurant was empty. She explains: "When we were paying the bill, I asked the staff when the crowds would come. I was so surprised when they said that between the time between 1 a.m. and 3 a.m. would be their busiest time of the day. . . . I asked if families with children came to eat during that time and he said, 'of course,' like it was completely normal for children to go eat at restaurants at 1 a.m."[29]

Fast-food chains are also frequented by young men out at night, students on their way home from school, and mall shoppers. Burgers, pizza, fried chicken, and *schwarma*—spiced meat grilled on a revolving spit, sliced thin, and stuffed inside flat-bread—are favorite snacks. So are fancy coffees, corn on the cob, potatoes on a stick, and all kinds of pastries and sweets, including American-style donuts.

## Family Time

Going out to eat is only one of many things Saudi families do together. Like families all over the world, Saudi families work and play together. In general, young people do not have household chores. Most families rely on servants from Southeast Asia to take care of everyday tasks. Approximately 1 million servants work in Saudi households, with the average family employing at least one. In fact, some wealthy teens have their own personal servant who attends to their needs.

But that is not to say that young Saudis have no responsi-bilities. Since women must either be escorted by a male fam-ily member when they go out in public or have their guardian's permission to do so, boys—as young as five years old—are fre-quently enlisted to serve as an escort for their mothers or sis-ters. And since Saudi women have traditionally not been allowed to drive, teenage boys often spend a portion of their free time transporting their mothers, grandmothers, and sisters. Girls, too, have responsibilities. They help their mothers care for their father, brothers, and elderly relatives.

Saudi families also have lots of fun together. Desert picnics—complete with multicourse meals and dune buggies—are popu-lar; so is going on a short family getaway to a neighboring Gulf state. Wealthy families take ski trips to Europe. But no matter what sort of activities families do together, Saudi teens know that they can depend on their families to care for them, advise them, and support them.

# CHAPTER THREE

# Education and Work

Education is a top priority in Saudi Arabia. The king considers educating the nation's youth an investment in the future. The government allots about one-quarter of the country's annual budget for education. As Prince Faisal bin Abdullah, a member of the House of Saud, explains, "The king's message is that oil is not our first wealth. Education is. We have to develop the people now."[30]

This emphasis on education is relatively new. Public schools were not established in the nation until the early 1950s for boys and in 1964 for girls. Today free public education from primary school through college is open to everyone, but it is not compulsory. Boys may drop out at any time, and male guardians have the right to withdraw girls from school at any time without any consequences. But most youngsters stay in school. According to the Ministry of Education, more than 5 million boys and girls are currently enrolled in Saudi Arabia's public schools. As a result, 94.7 percent of Saudi males and 91.1 of females ages fifteen and older are literate. In comparison, only 8 percent of the total population was literate in 1970.

> "The king's message is that oil is not our first wealth. Education is. We have to develop the people now."[30]
>
> —Prince Faisal bin Abdullah, the director of the humanitarian Saudi Red Crescent Authority

Contemporary Saudi youngsters and their families understand the importance of education in determining an individual's future. Even though having an education does not guarantee that young people will get the job they want, it does give candidates an edge in a very competitive market, especially if they specialize in a field in which workers are in high demand, such as petroleum engineering, computer science, or health care.

## Getting an Education

The Saudi education system consists of six years of primary school (ages six to twelve), three years of intermediate school (ages twelve to fifteen), and three years of secondary school (ages fifteen to eighteen). About 94 percent of young people attend school for a full twelve years. Saudi schools are segregated by gender. Boys and girls attend separate schools, where they are taught by teachers of the same sex.

Although a number of new schools have been built in the last decade, many public schools are run-down and lack modern educational tools. Therefore, some middle- and high-income students attend private schools. Like public schools, Saudi pri-

The government controls all education in Saudi Arabia. Schools follow approved curricula from which teachers are not allowed to stray.

vate schools are segregated by gender. They are usually newer than public schools and have modern computer and science labs and high-tech learning tools. Graduating from one is prestigious. However, attending private school is expensive. Tuition can cost the equivalent of $15,000 per year per child. Still, many families believe it is worth the expense. As an article on the Middle Eastern media website Albawaba News reports, "The general belief among parents . . . is that private schools will produce a generation of better educated and more skilled students who will be the economic leaders of the future."[31]

## School Life

No matter students' gender or whether they attend public or private schools, their course of study is almost identical. All Saudi schools follow a national curriculum that is set by the Ministry of Education. Students in a specific grade study the same subjects for the same amount of time. Teachers are prohibited from offering personal opinions or deviating from the national curriculum in any way. And textbooks promote Islamic fundamentalism. According to sociology professor M.A. Nezami, "The curriculum is strictly packaged with a set number of subjects taught throughout the country almost in the same format and sequence."[32]

Students attend school Saturday through Wednesday, September through May. Schools are closed Thursday and Friday so that students can observe the Islamic holy day of worship on Friday. The school day generally begins around 7:00 a.m. with students reciting verses from the Koran, and it continues until about 1:00 p.m. Religious studies are stressed. Students spend an estimated one-quarter to one-third of each week studying the Koran. In the remaining time, they study Arabic, geography, history, mathematics, science, and art. They begin learning English as a second language in intermediate school. Girls also take homemaking classes, and boys take physical education. Starting in the 2017–2018 school year, physical education classes for girls were gradually introduced.

Students are assigned homework daily, and they are administered major exams twice a year. They must successfully complete a comprehensive exam to move from primary to intermediate school and from intermediate to secondary school.

Except for those students who attend special technical schools that prepare them for careers in agriculture, industry, or commerce, all secondary school students follow the same course of study during their first year. Thereafter, they are placed on either a humanities or a science track based on their grade point average. Top-performing students may choose the track they prefer, but lower-performing students are automatically placed in the humanities track. Students in both tracks study the same subjects each day but for different amounts of time. In all subjects, repetition and memorization, rather than understanding and autonomous thought, are stressed. According to Abdul Hamid, a Saudi student studying in Great Britain, "Western education teaches you how to think while Saudi education emphasizes learning by rote."[33]

## Little Freedom

Students are required to wear uniforms, which usually consist of a thobe for boys and a long dark skirt and a long-sleeved white blouse for girls. Girls wear their uniform under an abaya, which they remove along with their head covering once they are inside the school.

Students have little freedom during the school day. Generally, the teachers rotate from class to class while students remain in one classroom. Students get only two short breaks a day. The first occurs midmorning, when they are released to the schoolyard. The second occurs at noon, when everyone congregates in a common room for noon prayers.

Students are expected to obey their teachers and respect each other. Misbehavior is met with zero tolerance. Fighting can get a student expelled, as can using a cell phone during class. School officials have the right to randomly search students' belongings and confiscate anything they deem inappropriate. "Here's how it usually happens," Rasha Alduwaisi, a Saudi woman, explains: "A group of teachers or administrators, barge in a classroom, mid-lesson. . . . Then they start searching the desks and bags (Saudi schools don't provide lockers). No they're not looking for drugs!! They confiscate any non-curricular books, perfumes, lotions, hair brushes and music CDs and other such items."[34]

Girls are especially closely supervised. To protect students and teachers from illicit contact with unrelated males, schools for

## Women and Driving in Saudi Arabia

Males in Saudi Arabia can get a driver's license at seventeen, and many boys begin driving illegally before the permitted age. Females, on the other hand, have not been allowed to drive regardless of their age. A decree issued by the Saudi government in September 2017 showed this to be changing. That decree made it legal for women to drive beginning in June 2018. Until this point, the driving ban applied even to women who had a valid driver's license issued in another country. Conservative religious leaders insisted that allowing women to drive undermines social values. As a result, girls and women had to depend on a male relative, a foreign chauffeur hired by the family, or a car-sharing service such as Uber that employs foreign male drivers. Although Saudi females are prohibited from interacting with unrelated males, Saudi culture considers foreign drivers to be servants and therefore not a threat to a woman's virtue.

Being unable to drive was a problem for many Saudi women, especially those who could not afford to hire a driver or use a car-sharing service. Public transportation is unreliable, and females are not allowed on public transportation without a male escort. For these girls and women, if a male family member was not available to transport them, they were essentially trapped at home. Women's rights activists staged demonstrations advocating for driving rights—an effort that finally paid off.

girls are locked down. An elderly male guard is stationed outside the exterior wall surrounding the campus. He locks the entrance door at the start of the school day and does not unlock it again until the day is over—except in an emergency. Author Karen Elliott House describes the procedure: "The girls arrive in the morning and enter the school thru a narrow portal, which then is locked behind them. When school is over, the door is unlocked to allow the girls to be picked up by drivers or guardians."[35]

## College Bound

Approximately three hundred thousand young people graduate from Saudi secondary schools annually. Not all go on to attend college, but many do. There are twenty-five public universities in the nation. Students attending these schools do not pay tuition or fees, and they receive a monthly stipend from the government to cover their expenses. Youngsters are admitted to public universities based on their secondary school grade point average. Females must also have their guardian's permission to attend college. One teenage girl complains, "I'm currently struggling with my father and trying to make him approve that I go to medical school. It's my last year of high school, and I have no idea if he's going to approve that or not. I have no idea what my future holds."[36]

All Saudi colleges have separate campuses for men and women. The two exceptions are King Abdullah University of Science and Technology, which is mixed gender, and Princess Noura Bint Abdulrahman University, which is for women only. Men and women are not allowed to intermingle, nor do they have oppor-

Secondary school students sit for an exam in a government school. The grades these students earn during their secondary education will determine whether they are eligible to enter one of the nation's twenty-five tuition-free, public universities.

tunities to do so. Each gender attends classes in separate areas, uses separate campus facilities, and is taught by same-gender instructors. Girls are also instructed by male teachers via closed-circuit television. This method prevents the teacher and students from having direct contact with each other. Writer Rawan Jabaji recalls,

> When my cousin completed high school, she visited King Faisal University, one of the many public colleges in the kingdom, which has both male and female sections. She described the scene for me. At the university, women are segregated from their male peers, and even their profes-sors. . . . Professors lecture from remote locations and the women listen through a TV screen. And if a female student has a question during class, she alerts the professor by pressing a button below her TV screen and addressing the professor through a microphone.[37]

Most Saudi universities have modern buildings, well-stocked libraries, on-campus health care facilities, athletic fields, and access to cutting-edge technology. Students live at home whenever possible, but housing is available. Classes are scheduled around prayer times, and there is at least one mosque on every campus as well as dedicated prayer rooms with scheduled religious ac-tivities. Students can also participate in clubs and other extracur-ricular activities.

Students select their specialty or major field upon entering college. Some fields of study, such as Islamic studies, are more prestigious than others. Parents often encourage youngsters to major in these areas, even though they may not suit the require-ments of the job market. Indeed, even though there is a need for engineers and information technology experts in the kingdom, more than 50 percent of Saudi college graduates specialize in Islamic studies.

Women are not allowed to major in certain fields, including engineering, religion, and architecture. They are encouraged to study so-called soft/female subjects such as teaching, hospitality, and nursing. In recent years, however, more and more women are successfully specializing in mathematics, physical science, and medicine. Indeed, the majority of college graduates in Saudi Arabia are women, and women hold more advanced degrees than men. As one young woman says, "The fact that we wear long black robes, doesn't mean we can't think."[38]

Classroom dynamics in Saudi colleges are much like those in secondary schools. Instruction is in the form of lectures. Group discussions are rare, and students are strongly discouraged from expressing their opinions, especially if they disagree with the professor. "To criticize a teacher's arguments in a Saudi school is unimaginable," says Talal M. Alhammad, a young Saudi man. "It is not uncommon in Saudi Arabia for students to be completely silenced if they question the validity of a professor's argument."[39]

Many Saudi youngsters choose to attend college abroad. The United States, Great Britain, Canada, and Australia are among their top destinations. In fact, an estimated thirty-four thousand young Saudis are currently studying in the United States. Al-

Saudi students congratulate themselves on graduating from Gannon University in Pennsylvania. Many college-bound Saudi students seek out higher education opportunities in the United States and other foreign countries to increase their professional status at home.

though families worry about allowing their daughters to study abroad without a male relative to take care of them, more and more young women are being permitted to do so. A female student explains that "things are changing fast. Five years ago my parents said I could never go to the United States to university. Two years ago they said maybe I could go with my brother. This year they said I could go alone."[40]

Having a degree from a foreign university is a mark of status in Saudi Arabia. It also gives young people an opportunity to learn in a less formal atmosphere, sharpen their foreign language skills, and receive specialized technical training that may not be available at home. In addition, while living abroad they learn about other cultures and teach others about Arabian culture, which helps dispel stereotypes and fosters tolerance. In fact, the Saudi government considers these factors so beneficial to the nation that it offers scholarships to qualified students that pay for their transportation, tuition, and living expenses overseas. Ahoud Alqahtani, who studied at Marshall University in West Virginia, comments,

> "People criticize our culture and our religion. But we have made a civilized country out of nothing—out of the desert."[41]
>
> —Ahoud Alqahtani, a Saudi citizen

> I never thought I could get a scholarship to America. This is my first time here. I was surprised how friendly the people are, because I didn't think that they would be. . . . People don't know much about Saudi Arabia. My neighbor, who is a graduate student, he asked, "Are you riding camels at home?" . . . . I want . . . to give a good picture of Saudi Arabia. People criticize our culture and our religion. But we have made a civilized country out of nothing—out of the desert.[41]

## Getting a Job

Although having a college education increases an individual's chances of getting a good job, it is not a guarantee. According to the Central Intelligence Agency's *World Factbook*, in 2016 the unemployment rate for Saudi males was 11.4 percent. During the same period, the unemployment rate for all Saudis ages fifteen to twenty-four was about 30 percent. Many of these young people do not have marketable job skills. Due to the Saudi education system's emphasis on rote learning, they lack the problem-solving abilities needed in many jobs. In addition, many have degrees in subjects that are not useful for working in private industry. "They're just not going to have the dynamic, flexible skills that employers are looking for,"[42] says Edward Sayre, an associate professor of international affairs at the University of Southern Mississippi.

Rather than going through the time and expense of training their own citizens, many Saudi businesses hire skilled foreigners instead. Indeed, private businesses in the kingdom employ approximately nine foreigners for every Saudi national. Sixteen-year-old Haifa believes this should change. She says, "The biggest achievement for Saudi Arabia would be to get rid of the foreigners and hence solve the unemployment problem."[43]

Adding to the problem, some Saudis do not want to work in private industry even if they are offered a position. Many individuals prefer to work in the public sector. The government is the largest employer in the nation. Civil service positions offer high salaries; short, flexible work hours; and lifelong job security. Unfortunately, there are not enough of these positions to go around, and favoritism toward family and friends determines who is hired. For instance, members of the Al Saud family are automatically given priority when it comes to filling jobs in the public sector. Everything in the nation, according to writer Maureen Dowd, "operates on a sliding scale, depending on who you are, [and] whom you know."[44]

Finding a good job is even more difficult for less-educated individuals. About 50 percent of young people with only a primary school education are unemployed. Although some of these individuals qualify for manual labor, blue collar, or service industry jobs, many Saudis prefer not to do these types of work. Since un-

> "The biggest achievement for Saudi Arabia would be to get rid of the foreigners and hence solve the unemployment problem."[43]
>
> —Haifa, a Saudi teenager

## Saudization

To move more young Saudis into the workforce, the government of Saudi Arabia has instituted a program known as Saudization. The goal is to gradually replace foreigners employed in the private sector with Saudi nationals. As part of this program, companies are given quotas on what percentage of jobs must be filled by Saudi nationals. Since many Saudis lack the technical skills to work in the private sector, some companies hire Saudi nationals and pay them a salary to meet the quotas, but they do not expect these individuals to actually perform work.

Another part of the program makes it difficult for foreign workers to renew their visas when the documents expire. They are therefore forced to leave the country. With no other personnel, companies must turn to Saudi nationals. However, since most blue collar, service industry, and manual labor jobs are filled by foreigners, and many Saudis do not want to do these jobs, this presents a problem. Moreover, although Saudi Arabia has a minimum wage, it does not apply to foreign workers. They are paid about a third of what is required by law for Saudi nationals. Replacing low-wage employees with Saudis, therefore, puts a financial strain on some businesses.

Despite these drawbacks, the policy seems to be having a positive effect. More Saudis are taking on positions formerly held by foreigners. This suggests that more young Saudis will be able to find work in the future.

employed individuals are, for the most part, able to live comfortably on the economic support they receive from the government, many Saudis refuse to work in these fields. So these positions, too, are filled by foreigners.

## Women and Work

Women face additional challenges. Although a large number of women earn advanced degrees, many do so without a career as an objective. A lot of Saudi women prefer a traditional life as a homemaker. However, an estimated 34 percent of Saudi women who want to work are unemployed.

Females face several obstacles in the workplace. First, Saudi culture encourages women to stay at home. And even if they find a job, women are prohibited from working without their guardian's permission. Some conservative guardians refuse to grant it, preferring that their charges dedicate themselves to their home and family. "The minute a woman works she forgets about her home,"[45] says Abdul Karim, a young Saudi man.

Moreover, women are barred from working in many fields, including geology, petroleum engineering, and religion, among others. In almost all other fields, males are given preference in hiring. Maram 'Abd al Rahman Makkawi, a Saudi female studying for a doctoral degree in science in Great Britain, explains: "In Britain, I read every day about job opportunities at international companies like British Petroleum, Shell, and Microsoft, including companies with branches [in Saudi Arabia]—but over there, [these jobs are open] only to men. . . . I have been offered jobs at the ends of the earth, but in my own country, [the same jobs] are not open to me."[46]

Sharia law, which prohibits any contact between unrelated men and women, presents other obstacles. Some employers set up gender-segregated work areas to meet this challenge. But many do not have the facilities to do so. Also, transportation has long been a challenge and a big expense for working women since they have traditionally not been permitted to drive. To overcome these obstacles, many young women set up home-based businesses. They create jewelry and craft items that they sell online, offer other women interior decorating services, and design and tailor women's clothes, among other enterprises.

It is evident that young Saudis face many challenges when it comes to finding suitable employment. To help get more young people into the workforce, the government has established new policies that limit the number of foreigners working in the kingdom. It is also encouraging students to specialize in more marketable subjects. As Reem, a Saudi woman, notes, "Things are changing. It's subtle, but it's there and it's tangible."[47]

# CHAPTER FOUR

# Social Life

Like young people everywhere, Saudi teens like to have fun. However, due to cultural traditions and sharia law, they face limitations on their personal freedom. Any activity that may lead to unmarried or unrelated boys and girls interacting, from walking or sitting close together to casually flirting, is strictly forbidden. And venues such as cinemas, theaters, and nightclubs, where individuals might be tempted to act immorally, are banned. These types of venues, according to sociology professor M.A. Nezami, are "considered as sources of social problems and moral degradation, or even contrary to the teaching of Islam."[48]

Although these restrictions affect everyone, they are especially constraining on young women, who are forbidden from going out in public unless they are accompanied by a male family member or have their guardian's permission. In addition, they are discouraged from participating in athletic activities. As teenager Mintee explains,

> Life here for a girl is restrictive. You won't have the freedom to get in your car and drive to the mall, theater, disco, local hang out, or whatever. You can socialize all you want with female friends, and go to their houses and have all female parties, but no boys allowed. You cannot date here and if seen or caught flirting with boys in public, you can get reprimanded by the religious police.[49]

Yet despite limitations on their personal freedom, Saudi teens still manage to have fun. "It might seem somewhat boring for a teen," Mintee says, "but if you can make life out of nothing, socialize in a good moral way, you can find fun."[50]

Like all young people, Saudi girls enjoy having fun and spending time with friends. However, religious law dictates that girls in Saudi Arabia are only allowed to socialize freely with female friends.

## Friends

Saudis hold friendship in high regard. Friendships are almost always between young people of the same gender and often between extended family members. Friends are extremely loyal to each other, and friendships that are formed in childhood typically last a lifetime. According to author Nicholas Buchele, "Once a friendship has been built, it is difficult to undo and can survive disappointments and betrayals that would swiftly end in the West. . . . A wrong you have done a friend (or had done to you) will simply be forgotten. After an appropriate interval for sulking, you can suddenly find yourself embraced as if nothing had happened."[51]

Indeed, it is common for same-sex friends of both genders to embrace and show affection for each other. Friends often greet each other with a kiss on the cheek and hold hands while walking together. Such public displays of affection are not considered sexual in nature; rather, they are a way for friends to show fondness for each other.

Friends enjoy doing many things together. But all of these activities are segregated by gender. For example, young men enjoy hanging out in establishments that do not admit females. Groups of boys spend their nights in these places sitting on plush cushions, watching sports on big-screen televisions, chatting, drinking coffee, and smoking flavored tobacco from water pipes.

Female friends do most of their socializing at home. With their guardian's permission, they go to each other's houses, where they relax in the female quarters. There, they talk, snack on sweets, listen to music, play video games, and watch satellite television, DVDs, and YouTube videos. Young men also participate in these activities, which they often enjoy with friends in a spacious tent set up outside their home for just this purpose.

Both boys and girls enjoy attending wedding receptions. After a couple is married, the female guests and the male guests celebrate in two separate locations. Author Ann T. Jordan describes a wedding celebration she attended: "The two celebrations were in a large wedding hall, which was a rectangular building split in the middle so that it had two large, separate reception areas. To reach the separated celebration rooms, the men entered the entrances on one end of the building and the women entered the entrances on the other end."[52]

The bride's celebration is typically more lavish and raucous than the groom's. It begins around 11:00 p.m. and lasts well into the morning. There are usually hundreds of women of all ages present. Upon entering the reception hall, they remove their abayas and head coverings to reveal their best formal apparel. They visit, laugh, dine, and dance. As Jordan recalls,

> The women were dressed in evening dresses of all colors and styles. In the front right corner there was an all-female band playing Arabic music and in the front of the room there was a stage. Women were moving about and visiting and dancing. Some ten of them were up on the stage dancing to the music and others were dancing in the aisles. . . . The women at this gathering were having fun.[53]

Going to the mall is another popular activity for teens. However, to protect single women, some malls ban single men or establish specific times when single men can shop. Other malls designate separate floors for single men and for families, which includes single women. Since Saudi malls typically contain hundreds of upscale stores, all kinds of eateries, full-scale amusement parks, prayer rooms, lounges with big-screen televisions, and gaming areas, teens flock to the malls not only to shop but also for entertainment.

## Staying Connected

When friends cannot get together, they connect with each other and with the outside world via social media. "Everything to do with technology is a window to the outside world,"[54] says Hoda Abdulrahman al Helaissi, a female member of Saudi Arabia's Shura Council, a group of officials that advises the king.

Young Saudis seem to be on their cell phones all the time, and many have multiple phones. In fact, in a nation of approximately 28 million people, there are an estimated 51 million cell phone subscribers. Saudi Arabia has fast Internet service, and although the government censors access to some websites, it does not block social media websites. Many young people spend hours online each day. With 2.4 million users, Saudi Arabia has the highest per capita usage of Twitter in the world. Youngsters also connect on Snapchat, Instagram, and Facebook, which has over 5 million Saudi members. And they have apps for almost everything imaginable. According to journalist Ben Hubbard,

> "Everything to do with technology is a window to the outside world."[54]
>
> —Hoda Abdulrahman al Helaissi, a female member of Saudi Arabia's Shura Council

> For many young Saudis, life is all about their apps. They don't have free speech, so they debate on Twitter. They can't flirt at the mall, so they do it on WhatsApp and Snapchat. . . . And in a country where shops close for Muslim prayers five times a day, there are apps that not only issue a call to prayer from your pocket but also calculate whether you can reach, say, the nearest Dunkin' Donuts before it shuts.[55]

## Saudi Arabian Names

Saudi names may seem long and confusing to non-Arabs, but they are quite practical. Traditionally, Arabian names follow a chain that makes it possible for young Saudis to trace their paternal ancestry backward in time and identify their tribal connections.

Here is how it works: Every Saudi has a given, or first, name which is followed by the word *ibn* or *bin* for males and *ibnat* or *bint* for females; these words mean "son of" and "daughter of," respectively. This is followed by the first name of the person's father, which is once again followed by *ibn/bin* or *ibnat/bint*, followed by the first name of the person's paternal grandfather. The grandfather's name is followed by the family's surname. Some Saudis place the word *Al*, which means "family of" or "tribe of," before the surname. So the name Ali ibn Salman ibn Muhammad Al Jasir, for example, denotes that a man named Ali is the son of Salman, and the grandson of Muhammad of the Jasir family. Sometimes in names "al" can just mean "the" and then it is transcribed in lower case.

Girls and women do not change their name when they marry, but children take on the father's family name. So if Ali has a son named Yusef, Yusef's full name would be Yusef ibn Ali ibn Salman Al Jasir.

### Dating

As Hubbard notes, many young Saudis use their cell phones and social media to flirt. In a nation where the genders are strictly segregated, and it is illegal for unrelated members of the opposite sex to interact in even the most innocent manner, dating is forbidden. Individuals discovered socializing with a nonfamily member of the opposite sex face punishment that can include a reprimand, a beating, or imprisonment, and they bring shame upon their families. Some young people pretend to be siblings or married to go out in public together, but it is not difficult for the authorities to learn the truth. As Hassan, a young Saudi man, explains,

> Dating is complicated in Saudi Arabia. You have to be careful just talking to a woman, because if someone finds out, it can be a really big problem. So it's better not to tell anybody. If you want to go to a cafe with her, you totally can't. The police might stop you and ask, "Who's that?" If you say she is your sister, they ask for proof. If they find out she isn't your sister, they will take you to the police station.

If you are found guilty of khilwa—when a man and woman who are not family members are together alone—you can go to jail for a few months. You can also be lashed 100 times. Sometimes you're told that you have to marry the woman. That way you might not have to go to jail.[56]

To avoid this kind of situation, many young Saudis turn to social media, which gives young people a means to secretly get to know each other and to cyberdate. In fact, it is not uncommon for them to meet on social media sites where they can interact with little risk. Sometimes these virtual relationships lead to more

*Young Saudis use social media to keep in touch with friends and family. Some even use these platforms to skirt the strict laws that forbid young men and women from flirting or even talking. Occasionally real-world relationships arise from these secretive cyberdating experiences.*

serious real-world relationships. For instance, twenty-two-year-old Raqad met her fiancé on Twitter when he responded to one of her posts with a private message. Soon they were tweeting each other every day and sharing personal information and photos. Although they never actually met, they liked each other so much that he asked his mother to contact hers to arrange a marriage. According to an article by Hubbard, "The couple is planning a family meeting to make their engagement formal. . . . It will be their first time in the same room. 'I don't have any doubt that he'll marry me or is serious about me,'[Raqad] says. Why so sure? Her older brother and his wife met on Facebook."[57]

## Boys and Sports

When they are not occupied online, Saudi youngsters enjoy sports. Due to gender segregation and cultural beliefs, participation in many sports and attendance at live sporting events are usually male-only activities. Many women and girls enjoy watching televised sporting events in the privacy of their homes, however. And, the new King Abdullah Sports City in Jeddah includes a separate family section so that women (accompanied by a male relative) can attend matches.

Basketball, volleyball, table tennis, handball, and baseball are all popular sports. But soccer—or football, as it is known in Saudi Arabia—is far and away the national favorite. Saudis are passionate about soccer. Men and boys play the game everywhere—on perfectly manicured fields located at sports clubs and private schools as well as in sandy vacant lots and dusty alleys. And they flock to the nation's many modern soccer stadiums. The largest, King Fahd International Stadium in Riyadh, holds about sixty-eight thousand spectators and is home to the Saudi national team, al Saqour, or the Falcons.

Most Saudi soccer stadiums are huge sports complexes comprising a main stadium surrounded by smaller sports venues that include indoor arenas, handball courts, swimming pools, racetracks, and playgrounds. But the main event is soccer. Fans, especially teenage boys, crowd into the stadium to watch their favorite teams play. Spectators can get quite raucous. It is not unusual for fans to throw objects onto the field and shout insults at opposing teams. And when the local team wins, the celebration

Soccer is the most popular sport in Saudi Arabia. Boys as well as men play pick-up games anywhere, from well-tended fields to empty city lots.

often continues outside the stadium. "They crowd the streets in their cars and indulge in such a frenzied merrymaking that traffic comes to a standstill for hours,"[58] says Nezami.

## Traditional and Modern Sports

Horse racing and camel racing are two other sports that Saudis enjoy. These sports are rooted in local tradition. For two thousand years Saudis have been raising, riding, and racing horses. In fact, Arabian horses are world famous for their speed and beauty. Camels, too, are a part of Saudi life and culture. These animals can survive in extreme heat, which makes them perfect for life in the desert. The Bedouin depended upon camels for transportation, milk, meat, and hides. Racing hundreds of camels across vast tracts of desert was, and still is, a main source of entertainment for Bedouin men. In fact, many modern Bedouin breed and train camels specifically for racing.

Although informal races are still held in the open desert, most modern races take place on special circular racetracks throughout the winter months. The most popular races take place in February during the two-week-long al Janadriyah National Cultural and Heritage Festival in Riyadh, which celebrates Saudi culture. Approximately two thousand camels compete in a total of ten races during the festival. More than twenty thousand spectators attend, cheering loudly for their favorite animal. Special family days are set aside when families, including single women, can attend.

For Saudis, camel races are more than sporting events. They are a reminder of the nation's past and a source of national pride. As an article on ArRiyadh, an official website that promotes the city of Riyadh, explains, "Such events reflect the cultural background of the local society . . . [and] help keep local customs and folklore alive, particularly for the younger generation."[59]

Equally popular, but less traditional, is a dangerous and illegal type of street racing/stunt driving known as drifting. Drifting, which is popular with young men, involves driving cars on public highways at speeds ranging from about 100 to 160 miles per hour (161 to 257 km/h) while tilting the car on two wheels. Drivers also spin the cars a full 360 degrees. Often, while all this is happening, a passenger stands outside the moving vehicle hanging on to the open passenger door with one hand as he slides along the road with his sandaled feet in an act known as the Saudi glide. Flash mobs of young men line up on the roadside to watch and record the action. The cars come very close to regular traffic, highway barriers, and spectators. Accidents are common. Saudi traffic authorities estimate that at least twenty people die each day in car accidents due to speeding, drifting, and reckless driving. Most are young men.

The nation recently made drifting illegal. People caught in the act can be fined and have their car confiscated for up to three months. Passengers and spectators can also be fined. However, the law has not lessened enthusiasm for the sport. To address public safety, some individuals are exploring the idea of creating arenas dedicated to drifting. As one drifter explains, "Drifting is fun. . . . The element of adventure and a desire to copy what I see in Hollywood movies in real life made me [want] to do it even more. Also, the feeling of breaking rules and driving without restrictions is what brings all the fun."[60]

> "Drifting is fun. . . . The element of adventure and a desire to copy what I see in Hollywood movies in real life made me [want] to do it even more."[60]
>
> —A young Saudi man who practices drifting

## Physical Activity and Females

Whereas drifting puts young men in harm's way, a lack of physical activity puts Saudi females at risk. Saudi culture and religious law discourages, and even in some cases prohibits, females from participating in sports or other physical activity. As Prince Fahad bin Jalawi Al Saud, a consultant to the Saudi Olympic Committee, explains, "Our society can be very conservative. It has a hard time accepting that women can compete in sports."[61]

In fact, until the 2017–2018 school year, girls were not allowed to receive physical education in school. And before 2017, they were forbidden from riding bicycles. They are now allowed to do so in parks. But they must wear an abaya and head covering and be accompanied by a male relative.

> "Our society can be very conservative. It has a hard time accepting that women can compete in sports."[61]
>
> —Prince Fahad bin Jalawi Al Saud, a consultant to the Saudi Olympic Committee

Females have limited access to other types of exercise. Although the nation boasts many well-equipped private gyms and sports clubs for men, it is very difficult to obtain a license to open similar facilities for women. Consequently, these types of facilities are almost nonexistent. In addition, public pools and tennis courts are open only to men and boys, as are swimming pools in most hotels. For example, when Reuters editor Arlene Getz stayed in an upscale hotel in Riyadh, she wanted to use the hotel's pool and gym but was turned away. She recalls, "As a woman, I wasn't even allowed to look at them ('there are men in swimsuits there,' a hotel staffer told me with horror)—let alone use them."[62]

This lack of physical activity can lead to many health issues for Saudi women. Obesity, for example, is a problem. Approximately 70 percent of all Saudis are overweight or obese. Of these people, 44 percent are women and girls. Obesity is linked to heart disease and diabetes. Fifty percent of deaths in Saudi Arabia result from these diseases.

Some Saudis are working to make it easier for women to be physically active, thereby improving their health and well-being. Some girls have formed basketball and soccer teams. Even though these teams must practice and play in private and cannot

## The Janadriyah National Culture and Heritage Festival

In addition to hosting camel races, the annual Janadriyah National Culture and Heritage Festival provides young Saudis with lots of other entertainment. The two-week-long annual festival is held at a huge fairground outside of Riyadh. It draws hundreds of thousands of visitors, many of whom are teenagers. The goal of the festival is to make young Saudis aware of and proud of the nation's cultural heritage. Najet A Louhichi, an editor of a Saudi media company, explains that the festival is "a great link between the past and the present. . . . We want our kids to be modern and developed. But we want them to know who we are. We want them to keep our identity."

Elaborate pavilions built in different architectural styles house different exhibits, including displays of traditional handicrafts such as jewelry designed to keep away the so-called evil eye, costumes, and food. There are also performances of traditional songs and poems, storytelling, and dances, including a male sword dance. Lectures on topical issues, such as Saudi Arabia's role in the world or how to combat terrorism, are held. In keeping with cultural practices, eight days of the festival are family days, in which families and single women can attend. The remaining days are only for males.

Quoted in Caryle Murphy, "Saudi's Cultural Colossus Attracts 600,000 to Former Camel Race," *National* (Abu Dhabi), March 26, 2010. www.thenational.ae.

participate in state-organized sports leagues, they are growing in popularity. In addition, the government has promised to issue more licenses to female-only gyms. The goal is to have a women's gym in every neighborhood. As Deborah Parkwood, the head of a women's basketball team in the port city of Jeddah, explains, "We have great athletes here in Saudi Arabia. . . . The girls, they want to play harder, they want to train harder."[63]

Both Saudi boys and girls face limitations on what they can do for recreation. However, no matter what limitations are placed on them, young Saudis still manage to enjoy life while respecting their culture and traditions.

# CHAPTER FIVE

# A Deeply Religious Society

Religion dominates almost every aspect of daily life in Saudi Arabia and, for the most part, determines how people behave. One hundred percent of Saudis identify as Muslims, and many are devout. Islam is the state religion. Saudi Arabia has no freedom of religion; non-Muslim places of worship, holy books, and religious symbols are illegal. And converting from Islam to another religion is punishable by death. The nation's constitution is based on the Koran, and the king is the official guardian and protector of Islam's two holiest sites. Being the home of these sites and the birthplace of Islam gives the nation great importance to Muslims all over the world. Indeed, the Sacred Mosque is so revered by Muslims that no matter their location, they face in the direction of Mecca when they pray.

Most Saudis are proud of the role they play in the Muslim world. Many believe that their strict religious society serves as an example of an ideal Muslim nation. "We are the spring of Islam and it's inevitable that we are different from others in our values and religion,"[64] Aljazi al Shebaiki, a retired female university professor, explains.

Saudis rely on the five pillars of Islam to guide their daily lives. These are a set of five rules of faith that all Muslims are expected to follow. As soon as they are old enough to understand, Saudi children are taught to respect and obey these rules. The first pillar requires that believers formally declare their faith, which Muslims do in their prayers. The second pillar requires that Muslims pray five times a day—at dawn, noon, afternoon, evening, and night. From the age of seven, youngsters begin performing this obligation. The wail of muezzins, or criers, summoning people to prayer through loudspeakers mounted on mosques is a common sound, and daily life revolves around prayer times. During these times, almost all other activity comes to a standstill. Stores, banks, restaurants, and gas stations close so that everyone can pray. Students in schools and workers in businesses stop whatever they are doing to pray. It is common for drivers to stop their cars and prostrate themselves on the side of the road to pray. In fact, most new cars are equipped with prayer rugs. And workplaces, malls, and public buildings have dedicated prayer areas for people who cannot get home or to a mosque during prayer times. According to author Ann T. Jordan, "The rhythm of life in [the Kingdom of Saudi Arabia] is created by the five daily prayer times. . . . Shopkeepers close their shops when they hear the . . . call to prayer. . . . Restaurants also close during these times. . . . This rhythm of Islamic time is experienced all over the Kingdom, and it is the rhythm by which people measure their lives."[65]

> "The rhythm of life in [the Kingdom of Saudi Arabia] is created by the five daily prayer times."[65]
>
> —Ann T. Jordan, author

Giving to charity is the third pillar. Saudi Arabians donate millions of dollars each year to charities all over the world. Young Saudis perform acts of kindness, such as caring for a family elder, as part of this obligation. The fourth pillar requires that all Muslims fast during the holy month of Ramadan. Youngsters are required to observe the fast when they reach puberty. However, some Saudi children begin observing the fast at age seven. The last pillar requires people to make at least one pilgrimage, known as the Hajj, during their lifetime to the holy city of Mecca. Most Saudis make more than one trip. They also make mini-pilgrimages, known as *Umrah*. These are not required by the Koran and are not as complex as the five-day-long Hajj.

## Religion and Sexuality

Religion influences the lives of young Saudis in other ways too. The Koran prohibits sex outside of marriage. Females age nine and older who are found guilty of having sexual relations outside of marriage face punishment ranging from a beating to execution, depending on the specific incident. Boys age fifteen and older face similar punishment. Although there is no law that sets a minimum age for marriage in Saudi Arabia, these are the ages that girls and boys are considered adults in Saudi Arabia.

In addition to facing legal charges, unmarried individuals discovered to have had sexual relations bring shame upon themselves and their family. Most young Saudis are conscientious about not breaking the law or dishonoring their families, and strict sexual segregation makes it difficult for couples to spend time together at all, much less to be intimate. Says eighteen-year-old Amina, "In Saudi Arabia you can learn to control your behavior . . . which is good."[66]

A Saudi couple walks hand-in-hand along the beach at the port city of Jeddah. It is more than likely that this couple is married because such seemingly innocent displays of affection are otherwise considered unlawful and shameful in Saudi culture.

Nonetheless, some young people are sexually active. Often these individuals have spent time in the West, where sex outside of marriage is more acceptable, and they develop more permissive views than their peers. Even though these individuals are followers of Islam, many feel that cultural traditions and religious laws should evolve with the time and that people should be able to choose what is best for themselves without the legal system or society interfering. Despite this, they are not immune to societal pressure. To protect themselves and their families, most of these individuals keep their sexual lives hidden. Doing so is especially important for sexually active women. Female virginity is greatly valued in Arabian culture. It is considered a sign of virtue, devoutness, and good upbringing, and it is a prerequisite for marriage. In fact, although it is not required by law, some men demand that a prospective bride have a doctor certify that she is a virgin before a marriage can be arranged. Without this certificate, if a bride falsely claims to be a virgin, the groom can have the marriage annulled.

> "It's hard to have a premarital relationship inside Saudi Arabia."[67]
>
> —Alhamduilah, a young Saudi woman

Boys, too, are forbidden from having sexual relations outside of marriage. However, since there is no way to prove whether they are virgins, it is easier for them to keep their sex lives secret. Nonetheless, because of the high stakes and the restrictive nature of Saudi society, most sexually active males conceal their actions. Many young men indulge in sexual activity only when they are abroad. As Alhamduilah, a young Saudi woman, explains,

It's hard to have a premarital relationship inside Saudi Arabia. I think a lot of young men and women chat on the phone and probably through the internet too, but it's very difficult to have any kind of physical relationship because of the culture and family. Also, it's not socially (or religiously) acceptable here. There are a lot of young single Saudi men who attend college outside of Saudi Arabia, and some of them do have relationships with women. Not all Saudis are religious, so once they leave it's easy for them to do what they want.[67]

## Contraceptives and Abortion

Proper use of birth control can help unwed couples keep their sexual life secret. It also lets married couples control the size and spacing of their families. If an unwanted pregnancy should occur, abortion gives women a way to terminate the pregnancy. The Koran encourages procreation within marriage, but it does not make any clear statements about whether contraception or abortion is acceptable. Saudi clerics are divided about how Islam views birth control and contraception. Some say that decisions about birth and death rest solely in God's hands, so contraception is immoral. Others say that using a temporary form of contraception, such as condoms or birth control pills, is acceptable if both the husband and wife agree to its use, but permanent contraception methods, such as a vasectomy or other forms of sterilization, are immoral.

King Salman agrees with the latter group, so temporary contraceptive devices are legal in Saudi Arabia, but sterilization procedures are forbidden. Birth control pills and condoms are available over the counter in most pharmacies. Other contraceptive devices are available with a doctor's prescription. Still, some unwed couples refrain from purchasing these items, fearing that someone will observe them doing so. Others lack knowledge of how to use these items correctly. Students do not receive sex education in Saudi schools. Most youngsters learn about sex and family planning from a family member or a friend whose own knowledge may be limited.

If an unwanted pregnancy occurs, it can be used as evidence against an unmarried woman in court. For this and other reasons, some females seek to terminate their pregnancy. Voluntary abortions are illegal in Saudi Arabia. Abortions are only permitted within the first four months if the pregnancy greatly threatens the woman's physical or mental health. But there are a number of rules that must be followed. These abortions must be performed in a public hospital, the woman must have the written consent of her guardian to have the procedure, and a panel of three physicians must agree that an abortion is the only way to save the mother's life or health before the procedure can be performed.

In light of these limitations, some young women travel to other countries to have an abortion. Those who cannot afford this option, or whose guardian refuses to allow them to travel, often

## Daily Prayers

Although Saudi Arabia has thousands of mosques, Saudis pray almost everywhere. It is common to see them praying at work and school; in homes, malls, and parks; and even on roadsides. Men and boys are more likely to go to a mosque to pray than girls and women, who are encouraged to pray at home.

Before starting to pray, individuals place a mat known as a prayer rug on the ground. Islamic daily prayer rituals are more physical than those in many other religions. Muslim prayers involve specific body movements and positions that are synchronized with specific prayers.

To begin, individuals stand facing the direction of Mecca, raise their hands up to their ears and say in Arabic "Allah is great." Still standing, they then place their hands above their navel and continue to pray. Next, while reciting a specific prayer, they bend into a position known as *raku*, with their hands on their knees. They then stand back up while continuing to pray. At a specific point in the prayer, they kneel down with their hands, head, knees, and feet on the ground. From this position, they rise up and sit on their knees to complete their prayers.

ingest dangerous drugs in an attempt to induce a miscarriage. However, if these medicines are used inappropriately, they can damage a woman's reproductive system or cause prolonged, fatal bleeding. As one Saudi woman explains, "I got rid of my pregnancy but I am now paying a high price to regain my fertility in order to be able to become pregnant again."[68]

Others seek out an illegal abortion. These procedures are usually performed by untrained individuals in an unsanitary environment. And if discovered, both the patient and the provider face fines and imprisonment.

## Homosexuality

Homosexual youths face other challenges. Islam forbids homosexuality. Under Saudi Arabia's strict sharia law, individuals found guilty of homosexuality face punishments that include imprisonment, beating with a cane, castration, or execution. To protect themselves, most gays and lesbians in the nation keep their sexual orientation secret. As Samir, a young gay man, explains, "I've been invited to private parties for gay men in Jeddah, but I never go because I know what would happen if we were caught. You can't let a word slip that makes you seem gay-friendly or gay."[69] Aside from the legal restrictions against it, homosexuality is generally viewed negatively in Saudi culture. Rania, a Saudi human resources manager, displays a common attitude when she says, "I disapprove. Women weren't meant to be with women, and men aren't supposed to be with men."[70]

Despite this attitude, the nation's strict gender segregation sometimes makes it easier for individuals to have homosexual rather than heterosexual relations. "It's a lot easier to be gay than straight here," says Yasser, a young gay man. "If you go out with a girl, people will start to ask her questions. But if I have a [male] date upstairs and my family is downstairs, they won't even come up."[71]

Moreover, local culture separates sexual actions from sexual orientation. Out of frustration or a need for physical release, some individuals secretly have same-gender sex because it is so difficult to have a relationship with the opposite sex. But many of these youngsters do not identify as homosexuals. As Yasmin, a Saudi college student, explains, "They're not really homosexual. They're like cell mates in prison."[72]

## Ramadan

Although Islam's influence is felt every day, it is felt most strongly during Ramadan. During this month-long holiday, Muslims who have reached puberty—and often younger individuals as well—fast from sunrise to sunset in an effort to purify their souls. Food and drink intake is limited to a predawn breakfast and a postsunset meal. Under sharia law, fasting is mandatory, and even foreign workers are prohibited from eating or drinking in public. Muslims who are discovered eating or drinking during fasting hours may be arrested.

Life in the nation changes during the holiday. Businesses and schools curtail their operating hours, and some shut down completely from dawn to dusk. Many Saudis either do not work or work only part-time during the month, and those who can do so relax and sleep during the day. Streets and roads are emptier than usual during daylight hours. But once the final prayers of the day are said, the nation comes alive. Many people stay up all night celebrating. They crowd the brightly lit and festively decorated streets. Stores and restaurants reopen and remain open until right before sunrise.

Families gather together for *iftar*—the evening meal—in homes and restaurants. Restaurants offer elaborate *iftar* buffets, and fast-food restaurants offer *iftar* specials. Many people snack all night to fortify themselves for the daytime fast. Shops run nightly Ramadan sales, and bargain hunters mob the malls searching for new clothes and gifts for their loved ones, servants, and friends.

The clothes are worn and the gifts are exchanged during Eid al Fitr, a three-day holiday that celebrates the end of Ramadan. "Basically, Muslims are done with the fasting, and are moving into party mode. . . . It is supposed to be a time of forgiveness and giving to those who are less fortunate. So kinda like the Christmas season for non-Muslims,"[73] explains Kristine, a Canadian blogger living in

Saudi children celebrate the end of fasting during Ramadan. The holiest month in Islam calls upon the faithful to limit eating and drinking and to refrain from sinful activities. Once the month of fasting ends, Saudis celebrate by holding banquets and watching fireworks displays.

Saudi Arabia. During the celebration, all schools and businesses close, and extended families get together. Children and teens are given gifts of money as well as beautifully decorated gift bags filled with toys, chocolate, and other presents. Wealthy people set up long tables outdoors laden with food to share with passersby. Others place large sacks of uncooked rice outside the homes of the less privileged. People who have disagreements are encouraged to forgive each other during the holiday. And cities hold huge fireworks displays. Young people go out to watch the lavish shows.

## Welcoming Millions

The Hajj is another holy event that has a huge impact on young Saudis and Muslims everywhere. One of the five pillars of Islam, the Hajj is a religious pilgrimage to Mecca observed for five days during the last month of the Muslim calendar. During the pilgrimage, participants retrace the steps of the prophet Muhammad. As

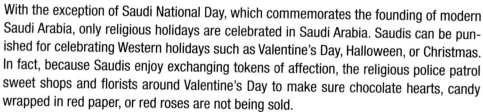

### Religion, Holidays, and Rites of Passage

With the exception of Saudi National Day, which commemorates the founding of modern Saudi Arabia, only religious holidays are celebrated in Saudi Arabia. Saudis can be punished for celebrating Western holidays such as Valentine's Day, Halloween, or Christmas. In fact, because Saudis enjoy exchanging tokens of affection, the religious police patrol sweet shops and florists around Valentine's Day to make sure chocolate hearts, candy wrapped in red paper, or red roses are not being sold.

Celebrating rites of passage such as birthdays and anniversaries is forbidden. But the birth of a baby is celebrated, especially if the child is a boy. Deaths are also commemorated. Saudi funerals are quite simple. When a person dies, members of the family, including teenagers, wash the person's body—with males tending to males and females tending to females. Then they wrap the cleansed body in a length of cloth known as a shroud. The body is taken to the desert for burial. Only men and boys attend the burial. Once the body is buried, nothing is placed on the burial site to mark it. There are no cemeteries in Saudi Arabia, and tombstones are rare.

Saudis believe that if they have lived a religious life, they will be rewarded when they die. So although loved ones mourn the dead, they also rejoice in the thought that the person is beginning a new life in paradise.

On the last month of the Islamic calendar, many Saudis undertake a pilgrimage, or Hajj, to the holy city of Mecca. Along the pilgrims' routes, fellow Saudis show their hospitality to the travelers by laying out food and providing other helpful services.

they do so, they perform a series of religious rituals that include praying, climbing hills, casting stones, and standing in place for hours. Many Saudis consider it the most important event in the nation. Each year 2 to 3 million Muslim men and women from all over the world, including about 800,000 Saudis, take part in the Hajj, making it the most populous gathering in the world.

During the Hajj, there is no gender segregation. Women and men perform these rites side by side. Almost everyone wears mandatory white clothes to show that in the eyes of God all people are equal no matter their gender or social status. It is a colossal event that evokes great emotion in the participants. 'Literally, the whole country mobilizes to provide generous services to the pilgrims, generally referred to as guests of God,"[74] says sociology professor M.A. Nezami.

Saudi Arabia's government spends billions of dollars on Hajj facilities. The nation is responsible for every visitor's safety and security—from moving several million pilgrims in and out of the airport in Mecca to providing them with public services such as sanitation, first aid, ground transportation, and access to telecommunications, food, and water. Approximately eighteen hundred police officers are deployed to Mecca during the event to provide overall safety. In addition, a massive tent encampment is set up north of Mecca in the town of Mina, where pilgrims spend one night in prayer. The final act of the Hajj involves the ritual sacrifice of an animal. To prevent each pilgrim from having to obtain and slaughter an animal, the Saudi government employs butchers to slaughter more than 1 million animals on behalf of the pilgrims. The meat is then frozen and distributed among the poor throughout the Muslim world. According to author and diplomat David E. Long, "Although many religions have pilgrimages, the Hajj is virtually unique in its worldwide participation and sheer size. It is hard for anyone who has not been in the Kingdom during the Hajj to appreciate its full scope."[75]

Although many young Saudis perform the Hajj, many others, especially those who live in Mecca, are employed by the government or by private businesses that provide goods and services to the pilgrims. Some young people share their homes with the visitors since many families rent out rooms to the travelers. Others sell the visitors food, beverages, personal goods, prayer rugs, and handcrafted souvenirs. Many work in the huge tourism industry that has sprung up in Mecca to accommodate the guests.

Those young people who do not provide goods and services during the Hajj, as well as those who cannot get to Mecca and participate in the event, observe it on live television broadcasts. It is a time of great peacefulness and joy for all Saudis in this highly devout nation where religion permeates every aspect of life. As Salman, a young Saudi man, explains, "Being a Muslim is most important to me, followed by being a Saudi."[76]

# SOURCE NOTES

## Chapter One: A Mix of Modern and Traditional

1. Quoted in Ann T. Jordan, *The Making of a Modern Kingdom.* Long Grove, IL: Waveland, 2011, p. 126.

2. Quoted in Mai Yamani, *Changed Identities.* London: Royal Institute of International Affairs, 2000, p. 43.

3. Jordan, *The Making of a Modern Kingdom,* p. 4.

4. *Kristine Wanders* (blog), "Saudi Arabian Overview," October 22, 2014. http://kristinewanders.com.

5. M.A. Nezami, "Saudi Arabia," in *Teen Life in the Middle East,* ed. Ali Akbar Mahdi. Westport: CT: Greenwood, 2003, p. 167.

6. Quoted in Kevin Sullivan, "Flogging Case in Saudi Arabia Is Just One Sign of a New Crackdown on Rights Activists," *Washington Post*, January 21, 2015. www.washingtonpost .com.

7. Quoted in Loring M. Danforth, *Crossing the Kingdom*. Berkeley: University of California Press, 2016, p. 2.

8. Jordan, *The Making of a Modern Kingdom,* p. 131.

9. Jordan, *The Making of a Modern Kingdom,* p. 127.

10. Oceana, "My First Day," *American Teen Living in Saudi Arabia* (blog), June 16, 2014. http://teenlivinginsaudi.blogspot.com.

11. Tiffany Wacaser, "Views from the Road," *In a Maze of Beige* (blog), April 1, 2013. http://beigemaze.blogspot.com.

12. Quoted in Mona El-Naggar, "'I Live in a Lie': Saudi Women Speak Up," *New York Times*, October 28, 2016. www.ny times.com.

13. Quoted in Ben Hubbard, "Social Arabia," *Upfront Magazine, New York Times*, December 14, 2015. http://upfront.scho lastic.com.

14. Quoted in Danforth, *Crossing the Kingdom*, p. 23.

15. Quoted in Yamani, *Changed Identities,* p. 19.

## Chapter Two: Family Ties

16. Quoted in Yamani, *Changed Identities,* p. 11.

17. Quoted in Karen Elliot House, *On Saudi Arabia*. New York: Vintage, 2013, p. 111.

18. Quoted in House, *On Saudi Arabia,* p. 77.

19. Quoted in Yamani, *Changed Identities,* p. 141.

20. House, *On Saudi Arabia,* p. 76.

21. Quoted in El-Naggar, "'I Live in a Lie.'"

22. Quoted in El-Naggar, "'I Live in a Lie.'"

23. Rasha Alduwaisi, "Rasha's Story, Part III: Marriage in Saudi Arabia," *New Agenda Blog*, February 23, 2011. http://the newagenda.net.

24. David E. Long, *Culture and Customs of Saudi Arabia*. Westport, CT: Greenwood, 2005, p. 35.

25. Quoted in Jordan, *The Making of a Modern Kingdom,* p. 52.

26. Nicholas Buchele, *Culture Smart! Saudi Arabia*. London: Kuperard, 2008, p. 108.

27. Quoted in Yahoo Answers, "What Kinds of Homes Do People in Saudi Arabia Live In?" https://answers.yahoo.com.

28. Buchele, *Culture Smart!,* p. 111.

29. Tiffany Wacaser, "Eating Out in Riyadh," *In a Maze of Beige* (blog), December 3, 2011. http://beigemaze.blogspot.com.

## Chapter Three: Education and Work

30. Quoted in House, *On Saudi Arabia,* p. 156.

31. Albawaba News, "Private Battles Public in the Saudi School System," September 7, 2000. www.albawaba.com.

32. Nezami, "Saudi Arabia," p. 174.

33. Quoted in Yamani, *Changed Identities,* p. 65.

34. Rasha Alduwaisi, "Rasha's Story, Part II: Educating Girls in Saudi," *New Agenda Blog*, February 18, 2011. http://thenew agenda.net.

35. House, *On Saudi Arabia,* pp. 152–53.

36. Quoted in El-Naggar, "'I Live in a Lie.'"

37. Rawan Jabaji, "Saudi Arabia's First Women's University," *Wide Angle,* PBS, October 31, 2008. www.pbs.org.

38. Quoted in House, *On Saudi Arabia,* p. 154.

39. Talal M. Alhammad, "The Education Dilemma in Saudi Arabia," *Harvard Crimson*, February 12, 2010. www.thecrimson.com.

40. Quoted in House, *On Saudi Arabia,* p. 154.

41. Quoted in *Time*, "Saudi Students in Their Own Words," March 13, 2006. http://content.time.com/time/nation/article/0,85 99,1172774,00.html.

42. Quoted in Julia Glum, "Saudi Arabia's Youth Unemployment Problem Among King Salman's Many New Challenges After Abdullah's Death," *International Business Times*, January 23, 2015. www.ibtimes.com.

43. Quoted in Yamani, *Changed Identities,* p. 84.

44. Quoted in *The Week*, "Seven Things Women in Saudi Arabia Cannot Do," September 27, 2016. www.theweek.co.uk.

45. Quoted in Yamani, *Changed Identities,* p. 108.

46. Quoted in L. Azuri, "Public Debate in Saudi Arabia on Employment Opportunities for Women," Middle East Research Media Institute, November 17, 2006. www.memri.org.

47. Quoted in El-Naggar, "'I Live in a Lie.'"

**Chapter Four: Social Life**
48. Nezami, "Saudi Arabia," p. 177.

49. Quoted in Yahoo Answers, "Life in Saudi Arabia for an American Female Teenager?" https://answers.yahoo.com.

50. Quoted in Yahoo Answers, "Life in Saudi Arabia for an American Female Teenager?"

51. Buchele, *Culture Smart!,* p. 95.

52. Jordan, *The Making of a Modern Kingdom,* pp. 154–55.

53. Jordan, *The Making of a Modern Kingdom,* p. 155.

54. Quoted in Hubbard, "Social Arabia."

55. Hubbard, "Social Arabia."

56. Hassan, "Sex and the Saudi," *New York Times*, January 8, 2016. www.nytimes.com.

57. Quoted in Hubbard, "Social Arabia."

58. Nezami, "Saudi Arabia," p. 176.

59. ArRiyadh, "Camel Racing," November 21, 2016. www.arri yadh.com.

60. Quoted in Adele Albanawi, "Fanatics of Motor Sports," *Saudi Gazette*, February 4, 2017. http://saudigazette.com.sa.

61. Quoted in Julia Case Levine, "Saudi Arabia Lets Women Compete in the Olympics, but Bans Them from Playing Sports Back Home," Quartz, August 8, 2016. https://qz.com.

62. Quoted in *The Week,* "Seven Things Women in Saudi Arabia Cannot Do."

63. Quoted in Marsha James, "Saudi Arabian Women's Sports Break Stereotypes," Learning English, February 9, 2016. https://learningenglish.voanews.com.

## Chapter Five: A Deeply Religious Society

64. Quoted in Donna Abu-Nasar, "Saudis Cling to Tradition," *Businessweek*, June 21, 2017. www.bloomberg.com.

65. Jordan, *The Making of a Modern Kingdom,* p. 137.

66. Quoted in Yamani, *Changed Identities,* p. 23.

67. Alhamduilah, "Do Saudis Have Premarital Sex?," Yahoo Answers. https://answers.yahoo.com.

68. Quoted in Albawaba News, "Underground Abortion in Saudi Arabia," May 14, 2014. www.albawaba.com.

69. Quoted in Lora Moftah, "'Gay Parties' Raided in Saudi Arabia; Religious Police Arrest Several People on Suspicion of Ho-

mosexuality," *International Business Times*, June 15, 2015. www.ibtimes.com.

70. Quoted in Nadya Labi, "The Kingdom in the Closet," *Atlantic*, May 2007. www.theatlantic.com.
71. Quoted in Labi, "The Kingdom in the Closet."
72. Quoted in Labi, "The Kingdom in the Closet."
73. *Kristine Wanders* (blog), "Happy Happy Eid," July 19, 2015. http://kristinewanders.com.
74. Nezami, "Saudi Arabia," p. 178.
75. David E. Long, "The Hajj and Its Impact on Saudi Arabia and the Muslim World," Saudi-US Relations Information Service, November 4, 2011. http://susris.com.
76. Quoted in Yamani, *Changed Identities*, p. 14.

# FOR FURTHER RESEARCH

## Books
Hunt Janin, *Saudi Arabia.* New York: Cavendish Square, 2014.

Susan Katz Keating, *Major Nations of the Modern Middle East: Saudi Arabia*. Broomall, PA: Mason Crest, 2015.

Megan Kopp, *Saudi Arabia*. New York: AV2 Weigl, 2014.

Manal al-Sharif, *Daring to Drive.* New York: Simon & Schuster, 2017.

Nel Yomtov, *Saudi Arabia*. New York: Scholastic, 2014.

## Internet Sources
Central Intelligence Agency, "Middle East: Saudi Arabia," *World Factbook,* 2016. www.cia.gov/library/publications/resources/the -world-factbook/geos/sa.html.

Fact Monster, "Saudi Arabia." www.factmonster.com/encyclo pedia/places/asia/arabian-peninsula-political-geography/saudi -arabia.

Donie O'Sullivan, "The Women Tweeting for Their Freedom in Saudi Arabia," CNN, September 16, 2016. www.cnn.com/2016/09/16 /world/saudi-arabia-male-guardianship-campaign.

## Websites
**Arabia Now** (www.arabianow.org). This website presents a wide range of articles related to Saudi culture, life, business, and gender issues.

**Ministry of the Hajj** (www.hajinformation.com). This official website of the Saudi Ministry of the Hajj provides information related to the annual pilgrimage.

**Royal Embassy of Saudi Arabia** (www.saudiembassy.net). This official Saudi website gives lots of information about life in Saudi Arabia.

*Saudi Gazette* (http://saudigazette.com.sa). This English-language Saudi newspaper offers a wealth of articles related to every aspect of Saudi life.

**Secrets of the Kingdom** (www.nytimes.com/series/secrets-of -the-kingdom?mcubz=0). Part of the *New York Times* website, this series of articles examines Saudi life, government, religion, and politics.

# INDEX

# PICTURE CREDITS

# ABOUT THE AUTHOR

Barbara Sheen is the author of ninety-eight books for young people. She lives in New Mexico with her family. In her spare time, she likes to swim, garden, walk, cook, and read.